I0477969

Credit Disputer Secrets

"DIY Credit Auditor Training Guide To Challenge and Remove

Negative Information From Credit Report Entirely"

By

KYLE RANSOM

Dedications

All my family members and closest friends...
Beautiful wife and daughter!

All content ©Copyright material and published by Uply Media, Inc 2018. All rights reserved. This material can not be reproduced without permission/ ©Copyright 2023, New Update. This material may not be reproduced, distributed, transmitted, displayed, or published without the express written permission of Uply Media, Inc. The contents of this material are intended for informational purposes only and do not constitute legal, professional, or health advice.

Contents

Introduction

Session 1 Understanding How Credit Works

Session 2 Blueprint For What Makes Perfect Credit

Session 3 Credit Audit Training

Session 4 How-to Challenge Accuracy On Credit Reports

Session 5 Checklist Module

New Bonus

Credit Disputer GPT by Uply Media Inc.

The content contained herein is not legal advice and is not intended to be legal advice. This information is for informational and educational purposes only.

Introduction

Do you really need a better Credit Score? Would you like to learn how-to audit your own personal consumer credit report or provide this expertise as a service business for others to improve their personal credit scores?

Everyone could use Good Credit and learning these simple easy techniques can help you spot information found on credit reports to challenge negative information to be removed entirely.

Over 56% of consumers in the U.S. population are all living with Bad Credit. Having bad credit is damaging to lifestyle and financial happiness. Consumers with bad credit are unable to get the best interest rates and with low credit scores...They are only able to possibly obtain credit through sub-prime lending at much higher rates than offered to those with Good Credit. When consumers have bad credit, this will prevent them from being able to take advantage of the best or average interest rates to borrow money. Making it virtually impossible to live a very financially healthy and happy lifestyle because of the stress from financial instability.

Good news, Bad Credit is fixable! Just by identifying enforceable security interest, improper misrepresentation and poor documentation in credit report files. These are the top secrets used by attorneys, credit repair companies, and financial resolution services. When creditors inaccurately report information, no matter how small or seemingly insignificant this information is being reported inaccurately.

There are strict rules and regulations that prohibit creditors, credit reporting agencies, and collection companies from reporting inaccurate information.

Learn learn skills for how-to properly dispute negative information on credit reports. Through this financial breakthrough action plan start using rules and regulations best practices to remove negative information from credit reports.

Spot inaccurate information and learn necessary resources to dispute inaccurate information to remove negative data entirely.

This is vastly different than simply disputing an debt does not belong to a consumer for validation of debt. The dates of default are very significant when reporting consumer debt and especially when it comes to collections.

Many consumer credit reports contain collection accounts that can be removed entirely for violations of rules and regulations when disputed properly, using the right statute violations.

Understanding How Credit Works

The content contained herein is not legal advice and is not intended to be legal advice. This information is for informational and educational purposes only.

(Best Ways To Check Your Credit Report)

(Credit Report Secrets Creditors Don't Tell)

(620 - 700 Credit Score Rules Bonus: Blueprint For What Makes Perfect Credit Top Secret Bonus)

(How-to Boost Credit Score Faster Eight Insider Secrets)

Your credit report holds many paths for what kind of future and lifestyle you will be able to live. This information will train you on how-to evaluate and better understand the purpose of an annual credit report to achieve the best credit ratings. Resulting in living a superior lifestyle and getting the best credit rating results.

Best Ways To Check Your Credit Report

A credit score is considered to be the biggest part of your character when it comes to financial responsibility. Your credit score is evaluated using your personal credit history from your credit report and reveals many things about financial behavior stability. Things such as are you always timely or habitually late, etc. A credit report is often the deciding factor for hiring as well getting approved when it comes to rental applications, loans, mortgages, employment, insurance, etc. Which is why it is a very good idea to stay on top of your credit report activity.

Every consumer is allowed at least one free credit report from all three major credit reporting agencies once a year. While many companies offer services to pull credit reports for a fee. The best way to check your credit report is absolutely 100% free and you should not have to pay to obtain a copy of your credit report because of guidelines within the Fair Credit Reporting Act. Even if you already got your one free credit report for the year because credit agencies also will charge a small fee for a credit report beyond one free annual report. In fact, guidelines in the Fair Credit Reporting Act entitle you to a copy of your free credit report beyond your one free copy per year limit when certain conditions are present. In addition to accessing and checking

your credit report free of charge. There are also other areas about your credit report history that should be checked and reviewed.

Major Three Credit Reporting Agencies

Equifax Credit Information Services, Inc

General Inquiries

P.O. Box 740241
Atlanta, Georgia 30374

(800) 685-1111 Free, and when denied within 60 days.

www.Equifax.com/fcra

Experian National Consumer Assistance Center

General Inquiries

P.O. Box 4500
Allen, Texas 75013

(888) 397-3742

(866) 200-6020 Additional when denied within 60 days.

www.Experian.com/freestate

www.Experian.com/reportaccess (When denied within 60 days).

TransUnion Consumer Relations

General Inquiries

P.O. Box 2000
Chester, Pennsylvania 19016

(800) 916-8800

(800) 888-4213 (When denied within 60 days)

http://AnnualCreditReport.TransUnion.com

Check Your Credit Reports FREE

Visit www.AnnualCreditReport.com or call (877) 322-8228

Option 1

Order a free credit report every year once a year.

Option 2

Order a free credit report within 60 days of being denied credit, insurance, or employment.

Or

On Welfare.

Or

Inaccurate information because of fraud, including identity theft.

Check Your Insurance Records

ChoiceTrust's C.L.U.E Report

www.ChoiceTrust.com or call (866) 312-8076

ISO Insurance Services (800) 627-3487

Medical History Report

www.MIB.com or call (866) 692-6901

Check Your Employment History

Acxiom

(800) 853-3228 select option 3

ChoicePoint

(866) 312-8075

Check Your Tenant History

ChoicePoint Tenant History

(877) 448-5732

U.D. Unlawful Detainer Registry

http://Udregistry.com/tenant.htm

(888) 275-4837

SafeRent

www.fadvsaferent.com

(888) 333-2413

Review Check-writing Report / Deposit Account Data

ChexSystems

www.ChexHelp.com

(800) 428-9623

SCAN (Stands for Shared Check Authorization Network)

(800) 262-7771

Credit Report Secrets Creditors Don't Tell

There are many hidden secrets inside your credit report that creditors don't tell you. The most important factor is that your credit report history reveals the worthiness of your financial stability to creditors. Your FICO score is evaluated based on your credit report.

FICO is the most commonly used credit score and Creditors base billions of applications from FICO credit scores to assist with their own level of risk and credit scoring systems.

All three major credit agencies consisting of Equifax, Experian, and TransUnion have partnership relations to Fair Issac Corporation known as FICO. So, for example because of variances of information found on your credit report among the different agencies your FICO for one credit reporting agency might be different from another.

FICO Score Range

Your FICO score range is ranked from 300 being the very low to 850 being the high point. Where a FICO score range in the 850 mark would be superb credit which is considered perfect.

Why a FICO score is so important is because shares for Fair Issac are traded on the New York Stock Exchange. All sorts of assets are securitized that are sold on the New York Stock Exchange.

The following assets are securitized:

- Mortgages
- Student Loans
- Auto Loans
- Credit Card Receivables
- Lease Payments
- Account Receivables
- Corporate or Sovereign Debt

FICO scoring is the pulse of Wall Street "Stock Market" and driving force for the New York Stock Exchange. The financial industry is linked dependent upon FICO scoring. FICO operates as a for profit entity and have shares traded on the New York Stock Exchange (important to point that out again).

The results of your FICO score is directly driven by your credit report data.

Here is how your FICO score is calculated based off of the information found inside your credit report. This breakdown is significant because

it reveals how FICO reviews a credit report to calculate how an FICO score is determined.

Payment History is 35%

This involves your current standing for debts that you owe. Including your past payment history as well. So, 35% of your FICO score is based on payment history for how well you pay debt that you owe and past debt that you owed. Payment history accounts for the largest percentage of a FICO score. For payment history having no late payments on a credit report is what Creditors consider to be superb. What Creditors don't like to see on a consumer credit report are Bankruptcies, Civil complaints, Foreclosures, Wage attachments, Liens, and other kinds of judgments. When it comes to late payments Creditors are much more concerned about recent delinquencies in a credit report oppose to accounts now in good standing with a late payment a few years prior.

Amounts Owed is 30%

For amounts owed FICO score is considered based on the number of existing accounts you may have open right now, available credit that you can access to right now, and the total amount you owe across all these platforms. So the "High Credit" amount and the lower ratio between what is available to you and what you owe is ideal standing for FICO scoring. When creditors see accounts closed on credit reports because the credit limit is maxed out this often signals that the consumer may be a risk to miss or make late payments and is very reliant on credit beyond needs over necessities. Amounts owed is also very important because it is the second largest percentage of a FICO score.

Length of Credit History is 15%

Length of credit history for FICO score rates the total length of credit history and the average length of time existing accounts have been open on your credit report. Creditors consider too many accounts opened all at one time too risky on a credit report and a FICO score can be reduced deeply by this action. The length of credit history makes up 15% of a FICO score is considerably important.

New Credit is 10%

New credit for FICO score is the total amount of new credit that appears on your credit report. Having too much new credit at one time can hurt and signal risky behavior. Ideally, creditors like to see new credit accounts opened between six months or more apart. Creditors also prefer that consumers only open a few new accounts over a two year period.

Which is why quick credit repair does not work. Additionally, new credit accounts for only 10% of FICO score.

Types of Credit Use is 10%

The types of credit use for FICO score is made up of the mix between installment debts, revolving debts, types of charge accounts, etc. When it comes to types of credit use Creditors favor mostly credit cards and revolving debt on credit reports. Consumers with credit cards and revolving debt are deemed to be more responsible in the eyes of Creditors. Types of credit use accounts for 10% of FICO score.

620 - 700 Credit Score Rules

Creditors have different guidelines for how they determine what is a good credit score and what is not. However, many Creditors will want a consumer credit report to contain a FICO score typically anywhere from 620 to 700 in order for consideration and approval. Generally to qualify for an auto loan a consumer will need at least a FICO score of 620 to receive an fair interest rate. For an conventional mortgage loan with good interest rates consumers will need an FICO score around 700 for approval.

Blueprint For What Makes Perfect Credit

While it might be debatable what is perfect credit....There are many factors among those with perfect credit in the FICO score range of 850 to finalize a blueprint for what makes up perfect credit. This what is consider a blueprint formula for Creditors to define perfect credit in a FICO score 850 range.

Many consumers with a FICO score in the range of 850 generally have the following similarities.

- A two year history or longer of superb credit with not one single blemish on their credit reports.

- Anywhere from a total of three to four revolving credit cards with a minimum high credit line of no less than 10k and low balance on no more than two at a time.

- A minimum of at least one charge card.

- Tradelines that are at least six months old and one must be no more than three years old.

- Nothing derogatory found in credit report.

- Low amount of credit inquiries and only one to three inquires within an six month stretch.

- No less than at least one good standing installment tradeline consisting of an auto loan, mortgage, or student loan.

How-to Boost Credit Score Faster (Eight Insider Secrets)

The best way to boost credit is to continue to pay all your bills on time and don't over spend. Here are some major factors that can boost your credit score faster with impacting results.

- Get punctual on paying your bills. Even if you paid late in the past such as 30, 60 or past 90 days late. Changing your payment punctuality can boost your credit score resulting in every month making late payment history a thing of the past.

- Watch your spending by keeping balances low. Use no more than 35% or less of available credit lines. Before you apply for a loan pay down you debt to 10% or less. Keep credit card use to a minimum and avoid purchasing big ticket items entirely.

- Keep credit history reporting going by using old cards

every six months just to make small purchases and pay off quickly. Old accounts are vital to your credit reporting history and activity on old accounts help boost your credit score.

- Increase and improve credit limits. Make sure that Creditors are reporting your credit limit accurately on your credit report. Remember you don't plan to use this credit you just want to increase your credit limit to boost your credit score faster. Ask your Creditor to increase your credit limit. Here again, you are not planning to use the credit limit or max it out. The purpose is to increase and improve your credit limits on your credit report to boost your score.

- Pay off bad debt to boost your credit score. If you have home equity loans try to pay down these as fast as possible.

- Deal with collections on your credit report to boost your score faster. Seek to get collections removed from your credit report. Removing collections from your credit report will strongly boost your credit score especially before it reach the extremely damaging area of charge-off.

- When shopping for a loan keep all inquiries within 30 days or less. This generally allows for inquires to be treated as a soft pull oppose to a hard inquiry which will bring down your credit score.

- Correct errors and flaws on your credit report is the fastest way to boost your credit score. An error on your credit report would be any information that is completely wrong. According to the FTC as many as 42 million Americans have wrong information listed on their credit reports. Things such as wrong social security number, date of birth, identity theft, etc.

Flaws on credit reports are items that contain damaging information not favorable on a credit report. Such as public records showing tax liens, bankruptcy, judgments, etc. Such flaws like collections, repossessions, foreclosures, and so on can really harm a credit report. Errors can be detected and when disputed properly can be removed entirely permanently. Flaws like errors on credit reports can also be removed entirely when disputed properly.

Many credit reports contain flaws that are the result vastly of securitization documentation mistakes. These flaws are often being misreported and misrepresented on credit reports. However, many consumers are unaware of how to detect flaws on their credit reports or even how-to investigate their credit report for flaws that may be misreported or misrepresented. As a result massive credit reports contain flaws for payment history, amounts owed, length of credit, collections, judgments, charge-offs and so on. The consumer is harmed for many years because of these flaws that if disputed properly could be removed before seven to ten years, the general time allowed to remove negative information from a credit report.

Credit Audit Training

The content contained herein is not legal advice and is not intended to be legal advice. This information is for informational and educational purposes only.

Are you looking to assist others with auditing their consumer credit reports to get a better credit score? Would you like to learn how-to audit your own personal consumer credit report to improve your own credit score?

Everyone could use good credit and learning these techniques can help you spot information found on credit reports to challenge for removal entirely.

Lesson 1

Getting Started

The fastest way to remove negative information from a consumer credit report is by disputing negative information. To effectively achieve removing negative information on a consumer credit report the best defense is to launch the dispute in writing to the creditor and credit reporting agency at the same time.

Why?

#1. All credit reporting agencies are required by Fair Credit Reporting Act known as the "FCRA" to investigate disputes on consumer credit reports. Additionally, credit reporting agencies are also required to re-investigate disputes against inaccurate information on credit reports.

#2. Disputing against a creditor directly is a very strong positioning point for getting the negative information removed or settling the matter in a more favorable light.

FCRA 623(b)(1) requires that when the credit reporting agency notifies a creditor that a consumer disputes information they must do the following:

- Investigate the dispute and review all relevant information provided by the credit reporting agency about the dispute;

- report findings to the credit reporting agency.

- provide corrected information to every credit reporting agency that received the information if the investigation shows the information is incomplete or inaccurate; and

- modify the information, delete it, or permanently block its reporting if the information turns out to be inaccurate or incomplete or can't be verified.

FCRA 623(b)(2) and 611(a)(1) requires the creditor generally has 30 days to complete the dispute once received from the credit reporting agency. However, when the consumer provides additional information that is relevant to the dispute within the 30 days the creditor shall have an additional 15 days to resolve the dispute issue. Which the credit reporting agency has five business days to supply information to the creditor and must also give additional information provided by the consumer promptly to the creditor. When the creditor does not investigate or fails to respond within the specified time-frame the credit reporting agency must delete the information disputed entirely from the consumer's credit report.

Lesson 2

Dispute Process

The dispute process involves preparing an letter with details explaining the issues found from the credit report audit and **sent certified mail with return receipt requested** to the credit reporting agency and additionally to the creditor the same way **sent certified mail with return receipt requested** .

As a Credit Auditor your job is never to offer or provide legal advice about credit disputes. When preparing letters to give back to clients to send off to creditors and credit reporting agencies it would be a good idea to inform them that legal advice is not being given or provided as well.

Each credit reporting agency may have different or the same negative information that needs to be disputed. It is an good idea to dispute negative information found to each credit reporting agency where the negative information appears. If no negative information appears on the credit report at one credit reporting agency but does on another. It would be a good idea to only dispute the negative information with the credit reporting agency where it appears.

Lesson 3

Dispute Requirements

Every dispute must contain certain information to identity the consumer with the credit reporting agency. **Refer to the Checklist Module 1** to make sure that there are no delays and that the credit reporting agency have all the information needed to identify the consumer to launch the dispute investigation. When the credit reporting agency does not have all the information to identify the consumer the dispute is delayed and an letter is sent to the consumer to send in identification information to actually launch the dispute investigation.

Generally, the consumer must state the following for disputing information on credit reports.

Consumer's name:
Consumer's Social security number:
Consumer's address:
Consumer's date of birth:
Consumer's previous address past two years:
Account name and number disputed:
Detail inaccurate information disputed:

Credit reporting agencies contact addresses:

Experian National Consumer Assistance Center
P.O. Box 4500
Allen, Texas 75013

Equifax Information Services
P.O. Box 740256
Atlanta, GA 30374

TransUnion Consumer Dispute Center
P.O. Box 2000
Chester, PA 19016

Lesson 4

Dispute Time-frame

When the consumer requests an free annual credit report the credit reporting agency has exactly 45 days to investigate and complete the dispute. When the consumer does not receive an free annual credit report the credit reporting agency has exactly 30 days to investigate and complete the dispute.

If the dispute is not resolved it is a good idea to request an re-investigation detailing new dispute inaccurate information. The key point is to not give up until the negative information is resolved.

Lesson 5

Credit Auditing Setup

The best way for a consumer to order their credit report is by getting a free copy of their annual credit report from AnnualCreditReport.com .

Every year a consumer is entitled to receive a free copy of their annual credit report from all three agencies consisting of Equifax, Experian, and TransUnion.

Order a free credit report via AnnualCreditReport.com or call 1-877-322-8228. To mail off for a copy send to:

Annual Credit Report Request Service
P.O. Box 105281
Atlanta, GA 30348-5281

Complete the form to receive a free copy of credit report.

https://www.consumer.ftc.gov/articles/pdf-0093-annual-report-request-form.pdf

Never contact the three credit reporting agencies individually. By using AnnualCreditReport.com this allows to order a credit report for all three credit reporting agencies at one time. Consumer will have to know identification security questions. When the consumer is unable to answer identification security questions correctly the will be asked for data requested in Checklist Module 1 in order to receive a free copy of the annual credit report.

Lesson 6

Spot Items To Dispute

The Fair Credit Reporting Act's Furnisher Rule governs what information creditors can report and what can be disputed. When auditing a credit report you will be looking for information that is inaccurate to have it removed from the credit report entirely.

Accuracy

When information is reported by the creditor to the credit reporting agency all of the information must be 100% accurate. When a creditor furnishes information to the credit reporting agency that they know or believe is inaccurate this is an illegal defense under FCRA guidelines.

How-to Challenge Accuracy On Credit Reports

Using FCRA Section 623(a) (1)(C) information can be challenged for accuracy on a credit report. By pointing out the information is inaccurate as it relates to the origination, creditor, date, amount, delinquencies, credit limit, past due, etc. Under FCRA Section 623(a) (1)(C) challenging that accuracy details are inaccurate puts the burden of proof on the creditor who must then confirm all the details are 100% accurate and not inaccurate that have been supplied to the credit reporting agencies.

Challenging Corrected Updated Accuracy

Using FCRA 623(a)(2)(B) updated information can be challenged for accuracy on a credit report. By pointing out the information remains still inaccurate and the updated information is inaccurate. The burden of proof is on the creditor to supply corrected corrections and updates. Under FCRA 623(a)(2)(B) the creditor must furnish only corrected corrections and additions to the credit reporting agency and must furnish only correct information going forward.

Lesson 7
Items Furnished To Credit Reporting Agency

Creditors are responsible to report only 100% accurate information about items to the credit reporting agency.

Creditors must include the following items to the credit reporting agency.

Credit Limits
Consumer Disputes
Closed Accounts
Delinquencies
Furnished Items
Under Appendix A (1)

The creditor must provide the consumer's credit limit with the information furnished to the credit reporting agency.

Under FCRA 623(a)(3)

The creditor must inform the credit reporting agency if the consumer disputes the information being furnished.

Under FCRA 623(a)(4)

The creditor must a furnish information on a regular basis and report if the consumer voluntarily closed an account and not the creditor that closed the account.

Under FCRA 623(a)(5)(A)

When a creditor refers an account for collections the creditor must notify the credit reporting agency and report the delinquency within 90 days. The delinquency must start at the month and year the consumer's delinquency occurred resulting in being referred to collections.

Under FCRA 623(a)(5)(A)

When an collection agency reports an account to the credit reporting agency they must report the delinquency date given by the creditor. The delinquency date will determine how long the debt will be reported on the consumer's credit report. Which generally will remain on the credit report for seven years.

If the creditor did not report the delinquency date to the collection agency then the collection agency may establish and follow reasonable procedures to determine the date of delinquency from the original creditor or another reliable source.

Under FCRA 623(a)(5)(B)

If the collection agency can't determine the date of delinquency they must establish and follow reasonable procedures to ensure that the reported date of delinquency to the credit reporting agency is the date before the account was referred to collections or charged off.

Lesson 8

Calculating Delinquency Date For Dispute

Delinquency date is determined based on the consumer's delinquency and not the creditor's later actions. If the consumer becomes delinquent on March 2014 and the account is sent to collections on October 2, 2014 the delinquency date is March 2014 and not October 2, 2014. Setting the clock counting toward seven years when the collections will be removed from the credit report.

The delinquency date starts from when the consumer never brings the account current. If the consumer becomes delinquent in April 2014 and starts making partial payments over the next six months and never brings the account current. When the creditor places the account with an collection agency in February 2015 the delinquency date would be April 2014 because the account never became current and the delinquency starts from when the consumer was unable to bring the account current.

When delinquent accounts are transferred to different collection agencies this does not change the delinquency date. If the consumer became delinquent in November of 2013 and the account was placed with an collection agency on May 5th, 2014 and that collection agency was unable to collect. So the account was transferred to a new collection agency on January 3rd, 2015 the delinquency date is still November 2013 and does not change repeatedly.

Under FCRA 623(a)(5)(B)(ii)

Even when the delinquency date was never reported by the creditor to the credit reporting agency the collection agency must still establish and follow reasonable procedure to learn the date of the delinquency from the creditor. The consumer became delinquent some time in November 2013 and the creditor never reported the delinquency to the credit reporting agency. When the account was assigned to the collection agency and the collection agency establishes the delinquency date from the creditor the delinquency date would be November 2013.

Under FCRA 623(a)(5)(B)(iii)

In situations when the creditor never reports the delinquency date to the credit reporting agency and the delinquency date can't be reasonably obtained from the creditor or any other reliable source. The collection agency must establish and follow reasonable procedures to ensure the delinquency date being reported to the credit reporting agency precedes the date that the account was placed in collections, charged to profit or loss, or subject to any similar actions by the original creditor and the collection agency may report the alternative delinquency date to the credit reporting agency. In this case any alternative delinquency date must be reported as before the account was placed in collections.

Lesson 9

Time-frame Negative Information Remains On Credit Report:

Not Paid As Agreed and Late Payments

Accounts not paid as agreed shall remain on credit reports for a period of seven years generating from the past due date and ending at the current date not paid.

All late payments will shall remain on credit reports for a period of seven years. For revolving debt and installment debt late payments shall remain on credit reports for a period of ten years.

Collection Accounts

- Collection accounts shall remain on credit reports for a period of seven years generating from the date the account became past due.

Public Records

- Judgments shall remain on credit reports for a period of seven years generating from the date filed including paid or not paid judgments.

Bankruptcy

- Chapter 7 & 11 Bankruptcy shall remain on credit report for a period of ten years from the date of filing.

- Chapter 13 Bankruptcy with a status of non-discharged or dismissed shall remain on credit report for a period of ten years from the date of filing.

- Chapter 13 Bankruptcy with a status of discharged shall remain on credit file for seven years from the date of filing.

Inquires

- As a general rule not all inquires on credit reports are bad. Inquires are records of companies who obtained a consumer's credit report to review their credit file. Too many inquires is what is deemed bad for a consumer's credit report. Typically, inquires remain on credit reports for a period of 24 months.

- Inquires that do not harm a consumer's credit report negatively are pre-approved offers which shall remain on the credit report for a period of 12 months. Account monitoring and account review inquires do not harm a consumer's credit report negatively and shall remain on the credit report for a period of 12 months.

State of New York Residents

- Paid judgments shall remain on the credit report for a period of 5 years generating from the date filed.

- Paid collections shall remain on the credit report for a period of 5 years generating from the date of the final activity on the account.

State of California Residents

- Paid and released tax liens shall remain on the credit report for a period of 5 years generating from the date released and 10 years from the date it was filed.

- Unpaid and released tax liens shall remain on the credit report for 10 years generating from the date filed.

Checklist Module

Information needed to launch dispute investigation.
(dispute, fraud alert, security freeze, disclosure)

The consumer must state the following for disputing information on credit reports.

Consumer's name:
Consumer's Social security number:
Consumer's address:
Consumer's date of birth:
Consumer's previous address past two years:
Account name and number disputed:
Detail inaccurate information disputed:

The consumer must validate ID. To do this include and attach a copy of one item below:

__Valid driver's license
__Social Security card
__Pay stub
__W2 form
__1099 form
__Court documents for legal name change
__Birth certificate
__Passport
__Marriage certificate
__Divorce decree
__State ID
__Military ID

The consumer <u>must validate address</u>. To do this also include and attach a copy of one item below:

__Valid driver's license

__Utility bill with the correct address (gas, water, cable, residential phone bill)
__Cell phone bill
__Pay stub
__W2 form
__1099 form
__Rental lease agreement/house deed
__Mortgage statement
__Bank statement
__State ID

Accuracy Disputes Module 2

Accuracy

Under FCRA Section 623(a) (1)(C)

A creditor cannot under any circumstances report information the consumer has told them is inaccurate if it is, in fact, inaccurate.

Under FCRA 623(a)(2)(B)

The creditor must provide corrections or additions to the credit reporting agency. Going forward, the creditor must furnish only the correct information.

Creditor's must have policies and procedures for the following:

- must be appropriate to the nature, size, complexity, and scope of your activities;

- must be reviewed periodically and updated, as necessary;

- should ensure that information provided to a credit reporting agency is for the right person, and reflects the terms of the account and the consumer's performance on the account;

- require maintenance of records for a reasonable amount

of time;

- establish internal controls for the accuracy and integrity of information, such as through random sampling;

- prevent re-aging (inaccurately changing the date of first delinquency on a consumer's account to a later date) and duplication reporting, particularly following portfolio acquisitions or sales, mergers, and other transfers; and
- require updating of furnished information where necessary.

All Information must include:

- be substantiated by the creditor's records when it is furnished.

- include consumer identifiers, like name(s), date of birth, Social Security number, telephone number(s), or address(es); and

- be furnished in a standardized form and specify the time period it pertains to.

Furnished Items Module 3

<u>Under Appendix A (1)</u>

The creditor must provide the consumer's credit limit with the information furnished to the credit reporting agency.

<u>Under FCRA 623(a)(3)</u>

The creditor must inform the credit reporting agency if the consumer disputes the information being furnished.

<u>Under FCRA 623(a)(4)</u>

The creditor must a furnish information on a regular basis and report if the consumer voluntarily closed an account and not the creditor that closed the account.

<u>Under FCRA 623(a)(5)(A)</u>

When a creditor refers an account for collections the creditor must notify the credit reporting agency and report the delinquency within 90 days. The delinquency must start at the month and year the consumer's delinquency occurred resulting in being referred to collections.

<u>Under FCRA 623(a)(5)(A)</u>

When an collection agency reports an account to the credit reporting agency they must report the delinquency date given by the creditor. The delinquency date will determine how long the debt will be reported on the consumer's credit report. Which generally will remain on the credit report for seven years.

If the creditor did not report the delinquency date to the collection agency then the collection agency may establish and follow reasonable procedures to determine the date of delinquency from the original creditor or another reliable source.

Under FCRA 623(a)(5)(B)

If the collection agency can't determine the date of delinquency they must establish and follow reasonable procedures to ensure that the reported date of delinquency to the credit reporting agency is the date before the account was referred to collections or charged off.

Calculating Hard To Find Delinquency Dates Module 4

<u>Under FCRA 623(a)(5)(B)(ii)</u>

Even when the delinquency date was never reported by the creditor to the credit reporting agency the collection agency must still establish and follow reasonable procedure to learn the date of the delinquency from the creditor.

<u>Under FCRA 623(a)(5)(B)(iii)</u>

In situations when the creditor never reports the delinquency date to the credit reporting agency and the delinquency date can't be reasonably obtained from the creditor or any other reliable source. The collection agency must establish and follow reasonable procedures to ensure the delinquency date being reported to the credit reporting agency precedes the date that the account was placed in collections, charged to profit or loss, or subject to any similar actions by the original creditor and the collection agency may report the alternative delinquency date to the credit reporting agency. In this case any alternative delinquency date must be reported as before the account was placed in collections.

Dispute Request Obligation Module 5

<u>Under FCRA 623(b)(1)</u>

When credit reporting agency notifies a creditor that a consumer disputes information they must do the following:

- Investigate the dispute and review all relevant information provided by the credit reporting agency about the dispute;

- report findings to the credit reporting agency.

- provide corrected information to every credit reporting agency that received the information if the investigation shows the information is incomplete or inaccurate; and

- modify the information, delete it, or permanently block its reporting if the information turns out to be inaccurate or incomplete or can't be verified.

Under FCRA 623(b)(2) and 611(a)(1)

The creditor has generally 30 days to complete the dispute once received from the credit reporting agency. However, when the consumer provides additional information that is relevant to the dispute within the 30 days the creditor shall have an additional 15 days to resolve the dispute issue. Which the credit reporting agency has five business days to supply information to the creditor and must also give additional information provided by the consumer promptly to the creditor. When the creditor does not investigate or fails to respond within the specified time-frame the credit reporting agency must delete the information disputed entirely from the consumer's credit report.

Time-frame For Negative Information Module 6

Not Paid As Agreed and Late Payments

- Accounts not paid as agreed shall remain on credit reports for a period of seven years generating from the past due date and ending at the current date not paid.

- All late payments will shall remain on credit reports for a period of seven years. For revolving debt and installment debt late payments shall remain on credit reports for a period of ten years.

Collection Accounts

- Collection accounts shall remain on credit reports for a period of seven years generating from the date the account became past due.

Public Records

- Judgments shall remain on credit reports for a period of seven years generating from the date filed including paid or not paid judgments.

Bankruptcy

- Chapter 7 & 11 Bankruptcy shall remain on credit report for a period of ten years from the date of filing.

- Chapter 13 Bankruptcy with a status of non-discharged or dismissed shall remain on credit report for a period of ten years from the date of filing.

- Chapter 13 Bankruptcy with a status of discharged shall remain on credit file for seven years from the date of filing.

Inquires

- As a general rule not all inquires on credit reports are bad. Inquires are records of companies who obtained a consumer's credit report to review their credit file. Too many inquires is what is deemed bad for a consumer's credit report. Typically, inquires remain on credit reports for a period of 24 months.

- Inquires that do not harm a consumer's credit report negatively are pre-approved offers which shall remain on the credit report for a period of 12 months. Account monitoring and account review inquires do not harm a consumer's credit report negatively and shall remain on the credit report for a period of 12 months.

Additional Time-frame For Negative Information NY, CA Module 7

Special Additional Time-frame For Negative Information

State of New York Residents

- Paid judgments shall remain on the credit report for a period of 5 years generating from the date filed.

- Paid collections shall remain on the credit report for a period of 5 years generating from the date of the final activity on the account.

State of California Residents

- Paid and released tax liens shall remain on the credit report for a period of 5 years generating from the date released and 10 years from the date it was filed.

- Unpaid and released tax liens shall remain on the credit report for 10 years generating from the date filed.

New Bonus:

"Credit Disputer GPT by Uply Media Inc."

https://chat.openai.com/g/g-uyltYhaZs-credit-disputer-gpt-by-uply-media-inc

Credit Disputer GPT by Uply Media Inc is a specialized digital assistant designed to help individuals navigate the often complex world of credit disputes. Its primary function is to assist users in crafting effective credit dispute letters tailored to various scenarios. This includes providing interactive templates that can be adapted to specific situations, thereby simplifying the process of disputing inaccuracies in credit reports.

In addition to letter drafting, Credit Disputer GPT offers guidance on legal defenses. This feature is particularly useful for users facing creditor lawsuits or needing to understand the legal nuances of credit reporting and disputes. The GPT provides educational mini-guides on a wide range of topics related to credit reports, giving users a better understanding of their rights and responsibilities in the credit system.

Another significant aspect of this tool is its ability to advise on follow-up strategies post-dispute. This includes managing unresolved disputes and keeping users informed about the latest legal changes that could impact their credit disputes. Such updates are crucial as they ensure that users are always operating with the most current information and legal standards in mind.

Moreover, Credit Disputer GPT leverages advanced tools like a browser and DALL-E to provide current legal information and create visual aids, enhancing the user's understanding of complex topics. However, it is important to note that while this GPT provides extensive information and assistance, it does not offer legal advice. Users are advised to consult a qualified attorney for any legal matters.

Overall, Credit Disputer GPT functions as a comprehensive educational and informational resource, guiding users through the intricacies of credit disputes and related legal issues, with a clear emphasis on practical application and up-to-date knowledge.

Thank You!

www.ingramcontent.com/pod-product-compliance
Lightning Source LLC
Chambersburg PA
CBHW030036230526
45472CB00002B/544